RELEVANT

*"The senior's guide to remaining
relevant in today's modern world"*

2nd Edition

SHELDON DUBOW

Table of Contents

COPYRIGHTS

ISBN: 9798865972068

ABOUT THE AUTHOR

After having served in the Military, Sheldon Dubow
(Shelly) began his career with a major member of the New
York Stock Exchange. He later joined the Value Line
organization in New York and was appointed Executive
Vice President and Chief Operating Officer of Value Line
Securities, a division of Value Line and The Arnold
Bernhard Co. While at Value Line he created a sales
training program utilizing audio and video applications
called "Applinetics". The progress was sponsored by value
Line and widely used by Wall Street Securities firms. Later,
Shelly joined the Piedmont Capital organization in
California to head up their West Coast securities and
Insurance marketing operations.

There he was responsible for the supervision and sales
training of over 160 licensed securities and insurance
salespeople. As President and CEO of Tri-Star Oil & Gas,
he compiled a successful and documented record of
Investor profits before selling the company to a major, Oil
& Gas Company in Denver, Colorado. As an inventor,
Shelly created the board game of "Qumero" which he
licensed to Coleco in New York and Spears Games in
England and, at the same time, as a manufacturing

entrepreneur in the confectionery industry; he created The Beverly Hills Confection Collection, a unique gourmet chocolate product line along with an exclusive method of manufacturing it. Prior to selling the company, the award-winning product was distributed worldwide. At the present time, Shelly serves as the Director of Marketing at CNE Worldwide Logistics, one of Florida's premier transportation companies and as the originator of Medialine Interactive.com, a California-based online Digital Marketing business.

Throughout his career, Shelly has served as President, companies, which were diversified in several fields, including finance securities arbitration telecommunications, energy, manufacturing commerce. Shelly is also co-author of a number one bestselling book on Amazon, "Rise Above the Cloud with Digital Marketing". Now, as an active senior in his 80's, and as a professional jazz pianist, he has taken a serious interest in the world of senior living and the challenge of remaining relevant in this ever-changing world. He hopes this book can help seniors, both men and women, to remain productive, happy, and most importantly,

RELEVANT

INTRODUCTION

Aging is inevitable, but becoming irrelevant doesn't have to be. In today's fast-paced world, it's easy for seniors to feel left behind, disconnected, and unimportant. The advancements in technology and societal changes can make it difficult to keep up, and it's easy to feel like you're no longer valued in this new world. But you are still valuable, and you still have so much to offer.

This book is a guide to help seniors stay relevant and embrace all that life has to offer. It's never too late to learn new things, try new experiences, and connect with others.

In these pages, you'll find inspiration, guidance, and practical advice on how to remain relevant in today's modern world. From the benefits of lifelong learning to the importance of building strong relationships, each chapter is designed to help you live your best life and make the most of your golden years.

So, whether you're a senior who's feeling lost or a loved one looking to support an aging family member, this book is for you.

Let's embrace aging with grace, positivity, and a commitment to staying forever young. Aging is often associated with wisdom, experience, and a wealth of knowledge. But in today's modern world, being knowledgeable about past events may not be enough.

As society and technology continue to evolve at a rapid pace, seniors need to stay current and relevant to remain engaged and connected. Staying relevant means keeping up with the latest trends and technologies, learning new skills, and finding ways to contribute to society. It's about recognizing that the world is constantly changing, and adapting to those changes is crucial to living a fulfilling life.

As we age, it's easy to become set in our ways and resistant to change. But staying relevant requires a willingness to learn and adapt, to challenge ourselves and step outside of our comfort zones. It's not always easy, but the rewards are immeasurable. By staying relevant, we can remain active, engaged, and connected to the world around us. Staying relevant is not just about keeping up with the times, it's about finding purpose and meaning in our lives. It's about staying curious and open-minded, and embracing new opportunities and experiences. It's about remaining vital and alive, even as we grow older. For seniors, staying relevant can be especially important.

As we retire from our careers and our children grow up and move away, it's easy to feel like our purpose in life has diminished. But staying relevant allows us to continue contributing to society, to make a difference in the lives of others, and to find new sources of joy and fulfillment. At the same time, staying relevant can be challenging. Technology can be intimidating, and the pace of change can be overwhelming.

Ageism and stereotypes can make us feel like we're no longer valuable or respected. But these obstacles can be overcome with determination, perseverance, and a willingness to learn and adapt. But aging is not without its challenges. Health issues, financial concerns, and social isolation can all take a toll on seniors' well-being.

Ageism and stereotypes can make them feel invisible and undervalued. And the fear of death and dying can be especially daunting. Despite these obstacles, seniors can find joy and purpose in the present moment, as well as hope for the future.

They can cultivate gratitude for the blessings in their lives, connect with others through meaningful relationships, and pursue their passions and interests with renewed vigor. The gift of aging is not one that is often celebrated in our youth-obsessed culture. But by embracing the opportunities and challenges of growing older, seniors can create a life that is rich in meaning, purpose, and joy.

So, let's honor the wisdom and experience of our elders, and let's look forward to the journey ahead with open hearts and open minds. In the pages that follow, we'll explore the many ways in which seniors can stay relevant and engaged in today's modern world. We'll share stories of people who have reinvented themselves in retirement, who have found new passions and purpose, and who continue to make a difference in the world. We'll offer practical advice on everything from social media and technology to health and fitness, from travel and adventure to volunteering and mentorship.

And we'll provide guidance on how to overcome the challenges that come with aging, including ageism, stereotypes, and the fear of the unknown.

Above all, this book is a celebration of aging and the many possibilities that come with it. It's a reminder that we're never too old to learn, to grow, and to make a difference in the world. So, let's embrace our age with grace and dignity, and let's stay forever young at heart.

CHAPTER 1
SENIORS SHARE EXPERIENCE THROUGH WRITING

Writing is a powerful tool for seniors to share their life experiences with others. It can be used to document moments of joy, sorrow, and insight gained along the way. Writing about your life can help you make sense of it, preserve memories for future generations, and even provide comfort in difficult times. Here are some ways that seniors can use writing to share their life experiences:

1. *Write a memoir*: A memoir is an autobiographical account of your own life story. This type of writing allows you to tell your story in depth and detail while also providing readers with valuable insights into the world as seen through your eyes. Writing a memoir takes time but it's worth it if you want to capture all the details that make up who you are today.

2. *Start a blog*: Blogging is another great way for seniors to share their stories with others on the web. Whether you're

reflecting on past events or offering advice based on what you've learned over the years, putting words down on paper (or online) will allow people from around the globe access to your thoughts and opinions about everything from politics to pop culture and more!

3. *Create an online journal:* If blogging isn't quite your thing, then starting an online journal could be just as effective when sharing your stories with others (and yourself). Online journals give readers access only after they have requested permission from its creator. This might be better suited if privacy is important when discussing personal topics such as family matters or health issues etcetera...

4. *Write letters:* While technology has allowed us many new opportunities for communication there's still something special about receiving written letters especially when they come from someone we care deeply about like grandparents or other elderly relatives/friends who may not always feel comfortable expressing themselves face-to-face due age related physical/mental limitations etcetera. Letters offer them an opportunity not only to express themselves freely but also offer those close enough

recipient(s) a chance to look back fondly upon them long after they've passed away.

5. *Preserve history:* Lastly by documenting our lives we're helping create part of history itself which makes writing doubly important for senior citizens since much knowledge and wisdom accumulated throughout their lifetime would otherwise go unrecorded & lost forever without proper documentation.

For example, one could write down traditional recipes handed down over generations within families or simply list out lessons learned during various stages in one's lifetime; both these examples serve a dual-purpose preserving family customs & imparting invaluable knowledge respectively.

CHAPTER 2
SENIORS SETTING UP A
SIDE BUSINESS

Many seniors often set up online businesses to supplement their retirement income or to keep busy during their retirement years. There are several reasons why seniors choose to become entrepreneurs and engage in business activities. First, many seniors have the time and experience necessary to start a successful small business.

They may have spent decades working at an established company or they may have been involved in various entrepreneurial endeavors throughout their lives. With this knowledge, they can use it to create a profitable venture that will generate additional income for them during retirement.

Often, these retirees already have relationships with customers, suppliers and other professionals who can be beneficial as they launch their new endeavor. Second, starting a business provides an outlet for creativity and self-expression that is not available from traditional employment opportunities. Many seniors find that running their own business allows them to express themselves creatively while still making money on the side.

This can provide great satisfaction for those who enjoy being creative but don't necessarily want to make it into a full-time job again after retiring from one career path already.

Furthermore, having control over what you do each day makes setting your own schedule possible – something many retirees look forward too as part of the freedom associated with leaving behind traditional employment opportunities.

Thirdly, some seniors turn towards entrepreneurship because there aren't enough jobs out there that suit them or pay well enough for them to live comfortably on just social security alone (which isn't always much).

Starting up a small business keeps those individuals active by engaging them with work related tasks which can help mental health, providing extra income when needed like covering medical bills or unexpected costs associated with aging.

Finally, establishing oneself as an entrepreneur gives older adults greater independence than being employed by someone else. This allows seniors more flexibility when it comes down to making decisions about how they spend their time. It also allows them financial stability through ownership of assets such as property which can possibly appreciate over time if managed properly. Overall, senior entrepreneurs represent an important segment of our economy by way of economic necessity but, also lifestyle choices due to increased life expectancy rates worldwide.

Therefore, encouraging senior citizens to pursue entrepreneurial activities should be encouraged where feasible given its potential benefits both personal and on an economic level.

CHAPTER 3
SENIORS PURSUING INTERESTS AND HOBBIES

In today's world, it is more important than ever for seniors to pursue new interests and hobbies. Not only does this help keep them mentally and physically active, but it can also help them stay socially connected with their peers. As one ages, there are many changes that come with growing older some of which may be difficult or unwelcome.

Pursuing new interests and hobbies can provide a sense of purpose and can challenge the mind in novel ways and even create opportunities to socialize with others who share similar passions.

For starters, engaging in activities that promote mental

stimulation can do wonders for keeping the brain sharp as
we age. Regularly challenging ourselves intellectually
through activities like reading books or playing puzzles
helps us remain alert while learning new things about the
world around us.

Additionally, participating in physical activities such as walking
or swimming gives our bodies' much needed exercise while
providing an additional mental boost from endorphins released
during activity; these hormones are known to improve mood and

reduce stress levels.

Furthermore, by pursuing creative endeavors such as painting or pottery making, we learn how to express ourselves creatively while honing our problem-solving skills at the same time!

Addressing loneliness is another reason why seniors should take up new hobbies; research has shown that feeling disconnected from family and friends increases one's risk of depression significantly more than any other factor associated with aging, including physical health issues or financial instability.

Participating in group classes like yoga/tai chi/dance/etc., joining local clubs related to your specific interest area(s) or attending seminars on various topics provides an opportunity for meaningful interaction with people who share similar values. This goes a long way toward combating feelings of isolation, which is often experienced by those over 50 years old (AARP).

Finally, importantly taking part in leisurely pursuits offers an array of personal benefits ranging from improved self-esteem and confidence levels all the way down to increased life satisfaction overall! A study conducted by researchers at Texas A&M University found that individuals who engage regularly in enjoyable pastimes exhibited higher "well-being scores" compared to those who did not participate in any type of leisure activity whatsoever (Psychology Today). In other words: having fun matters! So why not make use of retirement years by picking up something you always wanted to try?

In conclusion: Senior citizens have just as much rights as anyone else when it comes to pursuing whatever hobby they choose. Whether it's hiking outdoors on weekends or crafting handmade jewelry pieces during weekdays or evenings...the possibilities are endless!

By taking advantage of available resources within their communities, such as senior centers that offer Lectures/classes that are tailored specifically towards older adult needs and wants, seniors will reap numerous benefits both emotionally and physically whether they decide to explore something brand new entirely different, or simply revisit old favorite pastimes once again after several decades away from them altogether.

CHAPTER 4

SENIORS PLAYING

PUZZLES AND GAMES

W hen it comes to keeping seniors active and engaged, puzzles and games can be an effective way to do so. Puzzles are a great way for seniors to stay mentally sharp as they provide them with the opportunity to problem-solve and think critically.

Games on the other hand offer a fun way for seniors to interact with others while also getting some physical activity in.

Puzzles come in all shapes, sizes, and levels of difficulty which makes them ideal for any senior regardless of their skill level or mobility issues. From simple jigsaw puzzles that require only basic motor skills, to complex three-dimensional brain teasers that challenge both logic and creativity; there is something out there for everyone!

By completing puzzles regularly, seniors can help keep their minds active which will help prevent age related cognitive decline such as memory loss or dementia. Games like checkers, chess or cards are also excellent options when it comes to staying active as a senior citizen.

These types of activities require minimal physical effort but still get your mind working by providing you with strategic challenges that must be overcome in order to achieve victory!

Not only do these games provide intellectual stimulation but they're also great ways for seniors who may not be able to socialize easily due to physical limitations or limited transportation constraints. Seniors find companionship through friendly competition with other players either online or face-to-face depending on the game chosen.

In addition to puzzle solving and game playing, another fantastic option when it comes to staying physically fit is joining an exercise class designed specifically for older adults at their local gym or community center.

Exercise classes geared towards this demographic typically focus on activities tailored towards maintaining balance, flexibility, strength training and aerobic conditioning, all important aspects of remaining healthy into old age! Furthermore, many gyms will even offer discounts if you sign up multiple members from one family making exercising together more affordable than ever before! Finally, don't forget about hobbies like gardening which can offer mental stimulation through plant care planning, which gives you access to fresh air outdoors. This is something we often take for granted yet has numerous health benefits including improved sleep quality (and quantity!), increased energy levels throughout the day plus decreased risk factors associated with conditions such as heart disease.

Overall puzzles offer an entertaining form of mental stimulation that brings people together - whether virtually or via digital platforms like Xbox or, Live PlayStation Network, which can be played offline at home around a table. Whatever works best within everyone's circumstances should definitely be explored further!

Additionally exercise classes give older adults access to professional instruction within group settings resulting in improved confidence amongst participants. So why not give it a try? Finally, hobbies such as gardening allow us to reconnect with nature. Just make sure you have the right tools needed for the job.

Seniors On Joining Groups or Clubs

As a person ages, they may find themselves feeling lonely or disconnected from society. Joining a senior group or club is an excellent way for seniors to remain engaged and active in their communities.

Senior groups and clubs offer numerous activities that benefit both the individual and the community. Here are five reasons why seniors should join a senior group or club:

1. Social Interaction: Senior groups provide an opportunity for individuals to interact with other people of similar age ranges and interests.

This social interaction can help reduce feelings of isolation, depression, anxiety, and loneliness which many seniors face due to reduced mobility or living alone away from family members.

Additionally, it provides opportunities to meet new friends who share common interests while enjoying stimulating conversations in a supportive environment.

2. *Cognitive Stimulation:* Participating in various activities offered by senior groups helps keep the mind sharp since it requires focusing on tasks at hand such as playing cards or board games, solving puzzles etc., all providing cognitive stimulation which contributes to improved mental well-being over time.

3. *Physical Activity:* Many senior groups offer physical activities such as walking clubs, yoga classes etc., that promote healthy movement with low impact exercises suitable for those with limited mobility. This allows them to enjoy some form of exercise without putting too much strain on their bodies thus helping maintain good health overall.

4. *Sense of Community:* Being part of a larger community helps create positive relationships among its members providing support when needed while also offering entertainment through various events organized by the group. Examples such as dinners at local restaurants, movie

nights, and game nights. These events help to create lasting friendships within the group itself.

5. *Wellness Benefits:* Being part of a senior group can have immense benefits on one's overall wellbeing, including better physical health thanks to increased motivation towards exercise and improved mental health. This also contributes to increased cognitive stimulation that is provided by participating in different activities offered by these types of organizations. This kind of activity helps decrease the level of stress by being socially connected rather than being isolated.

As previously stated, joining a senior group offers numerous benefits such as socialization, cognitive stimulation, improved physical activity levels, along with providing a greater sense of belonging. Along with wellness benefits, it makes it an ideal option for anyone looking for ways to stay connected and improve their quality of life.

Seniors On Attending Cultural Events

As the population ages, the importance of seniors attending cultural events is becoming increasingly important.

Cultural events are an opportunity for seniors to learn about different cultures, explore their own identity and develop a greater appreciation for diversity in society.

Through attending cultural events, seniors can gain valuable insight into other cultures and ways of life that they may not have been exposed prior to.

This knowledge can help them make informed decisions on how to interact with others from different backgrounds and increase their understanding of various social issues related to culture.

The human experience is enriched through exposure to different perspectives, beliefs and values which are often highlighted at cultural events such as festivals or art exhibitions. Seniors who attend these types of events will be able to get out of their comfort zone by engaging with people from diverse backgrounds by learning new things about the world around them.

This type of engagement increases empathy within individuals as it allows them to see how actions affect those, we encounter in our daily lives, regardless if they come from a similar background or not.

Cultural events also provide senior citizens with physical benefits such as improved coordination due to increased movement associated with activities like dancing or playing musical instruments associated with certain cultures' music styles.

Additionally, cognitive stimulation occurs when attendees take part in activities that require problem-solving skills such as puzzles presented at some traditional festivals or competitions involving skillful games like chess which are popular among many cultures worldwide.

Furthermore, there is evidence that shows participating in culturally enriching activities has positive effects on mental health since it encourages self-expression while reducing stress levels significantly according to studies conducted by experts in this field.

In addition, seniors should attend cultural events because it provides them with a sense of belonging within their community; being surrounded by people who share similar interests creates an atmosphere where one feels accepted despite age differences between members present at the event making it easier for older adults to feel included amongst other generations present there too!

Lastly but most importantly: these types of gatherings offer opportunities for intergenerational exchange where younger generations can learn more about traditions passed down through families over time, something we all need now more than ever given current global circumstances.

CHAPTER 5

KEEPING UP WITH RECREATIONAL ACTIVITIES

Seniors are often seen as less active than their younger counterparts, but this doesn't have to be the case. In fact, seniors can and should keep up with recreational activities to stay healthy and enjoy life.

The benefits of engaging in recreational activities for seniors are immense; they include improved physical health, mental well-being, and social engagement.

Physical activity helps reduce the risk of diseases such as diabetes, heart disease and stroke.

It also assists with maintaining a healthy weight by burning calories and increasing muscle mass. For those suffering from joint pain or arthritis symptoms, low impact exercises like swimming or walking can help relieve some of the stress.

CHAPTER 6
DISCOMFORT WHILE STILL PROVIDING AN EFECTIVE WORKOUT

On top of that, regular exercise has been proven to improve moods through releasing endorphins - natural hormones that make us feel good - which is especially important for seniors who may be prone to depression or loneliness due to living alone or having few friends nearby. In addition to physical health benefits, recreational activities also provide opportunities for social Interaction among peers which can lead to stronger relationships within communities of senior citizens something that is especially beneficial given many current restrictions on public gatherings due to COVID 19 pandemic measures.

A wide variety of group classes exist both online (such as yoga sessions) and at local community centers (such as line dancing lessons).

Moreover, there are plenty of outdoor activities available for those who prefer being out in nature including bird watching, hikes or fishing trips. These are all designed specifically with elders in mind, so no one gets left behind!

Finally getting involved in hobbies like arts & craft projects provides a great way for seniors to express themselves creatively without feeling overwhelmed by more demanding tasks such as painting a mural wall inside their home! Overall, recreation plays an essential role when it comes to ensuring the quality of life during their golden years. Not only does it give them access to much needed physical activity but also lends itself towards forming meaningful connections with others which leads to positive feelings and overall happiness too! With so many options available these days there really isn't any excuse why any senior shouldn't take advantage of hem all!

CHAPTER 7
SENIORS KEEPING UP WITH CURRENT TRENDS

In today's digital age, it can be hard for seniors to keep up with the latest trends. With technology and social media plays such a large role in our lives, it can seem impossible for seniors to stay current. However, staying informed about what is happening around them is important for their physical and mental health. Here are some ways that seniors can stay up to date on current trends:

1. *Use social media:* Many older adults may think that using social media is too complicated or time consuming but there are plenty of ways to connect with friends and family without having to learn all the ins and outs of the various social platforms.

Popular networks like Facebook and others have made connecting much easier than ever before by offering features like video conferencing, instant messaging, and photo sharing, which make communicating simple even for those who are not tech savvy. Seniors should take advantage of these tools to stay connected with loved ones far and near.

2. *Stay Informed:* There are many websites out there dedicated strictly to news stories specifically tailored towards senior citizens. Staying informed helps keep people engaged in the world around them while also providing an opportunity to discuss topics they care about with others who share similar interests or experiences. Additionally, subscribing to e-newsletters from relevant organizations or publications will ensure that you never miss out on any important updates in your area or industry!

3. *Take Classes:* Learning new skills has never been so easy thanks to online classes offered through universities as well as smaller learning platforms like Udemy or Coursera where students pay a fee per course instead of enrolling in a full degree program at once.

Taking courses directly (or indirectly!) related to one's field of expertise gives insight into modern day challenges facing businesses today. This is something invaluable when trying to compete against younger professionals entering the same industry later down the line!

4. *Attend Events:* Attending local events hosted by community centers or libraries allows seniors an opportunity to meet other people in their own age while also becoming familiarized with popular topics being discussed within their city/town/region. This makes conversations more engaging when catching up over lunch dates or dinner parties afterwards!

5. *Join Groups & Clubs:* Joining groups designed specifically for older adults makes meeting new people easy since members already share common interests due simply being part of this demographic group alone.

However, joining clubs based on hobbies such as golfing, gardening, bird watching, or something other, give members access to additional resources regarding recent advancements within those industries.

This gives everyone involved an edge over competitors who haven't been keeping abreast of developments taking place outside traditional means (i.e., magazines).

By following these tips above, seniors can easily remain knowledgeable about current trends while still enjoying activities they love no matter how advanced technology becomes!

CHAPTER 8
SENIORS JOINING VOLUNTEER ORGANIZATIONS

As we age, it can be easy to feel like life is passing us by. But with the help of local volunteer organizations, seniors can stay active and make a difference in their communities.

By joining a volunteer organization, seniors can find purpose and meaning in retirement or semiretirement that will help keep them engaged and motivated for years to come.

Volunteering provides an opportunity for social interaction among peers who share similar interests and values. Many local volunteer organizations specialize in projects that relate directly to their community's needs such as helping at food banks, participating in beach cleanups, or providing companionship services at nursing homes.

This type of work not only allows seniors to give back but also helps them stay connected with people around them while feeling valued and appreciated by those they serve.

In addition to providing meaningful opportunities for socialization, volunteering may have physical benefits as well. Studies suggest that volunteers tend to have lower blood pressure than non-volunteers which leads to better overall health outcomes over time.

Furthermore, engaging in physically demanding activities associated with volunteering may increase strength and endurance levels which could lead to improved mobility or balance issues later down the line. Finally, volunteering offers financial benefits too, especially when it comes time for tax season!

By donating your time instead of money, you are eligible for deductions on your federal income taxes (if you itemize). And if you belong to an organization where members receive special discounts or incentives due solely because they are part of the group, then those savings add up quickly. Plus, there are often free meals provided during service events, so you don't need to worry about spending any extra cash either way, making this one great investment all around!

Volunteering is more than just something nice to do; it has real potential impacts on our lives both now and into the future so why not take advantage? Local volunteer organizations offer a chance for seniors to become active participants within their own community while simultaneously reaping all sorts of rewards from doing good deeds. What's not to love here?! So go ahead: join today & get ready to start giving back tomorrow!

CHAPTER 9
SENIORS INVOLVED IN THEIR COMMUNITIES

S eniors can stay involved in their communities by participating in activities that bring them joy and fulfillment. There are many ways to do this, as stated earlier, from volunteering with local charities and organizations, attending community events such as festivals or parades, joining a book club or other social groups, taking classes at the local college or university, and more.

Volunteering is one of the most beneficial ways for seniors to get involved in their community. Volunteering allows seniors to give back while also helping others who may be less fortunate than themselves. Volunteering opportunities are available at many different levels – from working with youth programs, providing companionship services for the elderly or disabled individuals, helping at libraries or at animal shelters. There's something for everyone!

Not only does volunteering provide an opportunity for seniors to give back but it also helps keep them active and engaged socially which can help stave off feelings of loneliness and isolation that often accompany aging. Attending community events is another great way for seniors to stay connected with their peers while enjoying some fresh air outside.

Whether it's a parade through town on July 4th weekend or a festival celebrating local culture during summer months, these outdoor gatherings offer fun activities such as live music performances and food vendors that make it easy for everyone young and old alike to have a great time together! Additionally, these types of events provide an excellent platform where seniors can meet new people who share similar interests thus creating meaningful friendships beyond just family ties. Joining clubs like book clubs (or any other type) is yet another effective way in which older adults can engage within their communities.

Clubs provide members with access to engaging conversations about shared interests allowing individuals of all ages to exchange ideas with each other while building lasting relationships over time. This occurs not only among its members but also amongst those living nearby who might be interested in joining too! Furthermore, reading books together provides ample opportunity for stimulating mental activity, which has been proven beneficial when it comes to combating age-related cognitive decline.

Classes offered by local colleges/universities represent yet another avenue whereby older adults can maintain involvement within their respective communities. This can give seniors an opportunity to opt-in towards earning a special certificate aimed at teaching. Whatever route chosen; knowledge/skills acquired will always remain useful both now and later down life's journey ahead!

Finally educational institutions serve double duty here since they typically host various lectures & seminars open free to public attendance.

If finances become an issue, then chances still exist that attending will still be possible without having to worry about tuition costs associated with traditional classroom settings! In summary, staying involved within one's own community provides numerous benefits ranging from improved physical health due to increased exposure outdoors via volunteer work/attendance at special events and enhanced mental wellbeing resulting from tighter social networks formed between peers. but they're also great ways for seniors who may not be able to socialize easily due to physical limitations or limitations on transportation constraints that seniors may find themselves in.

CHAPTER 10
INVESTING IN HEALTH AND WELLNESS PROGRAMS

Seniors should invest in health and wellness programs to ensure they remain healthy, active, and independent. These programs can help them stay mentally and physically fit while also providing social interaction with other seniors.

Investing in health and wellness programs is a great way for seniors to stay healthy, reduce their risk of diseases such as diabetes or heart disease, maintain an independent lifestyle, and enjoy a higher quality of life.

Healthy eating is one key component for a successful health and wellness program for seniors. Eating nutritious meals that are low in sugar, fat, salt, cholesterol can help improve overall health while reducing the risk of chronic illnesses such as diabetes or hypertension.

In addition to following a balanced diet plan with plenty of fruits and vegetables as well as lean proteins like fish or poultry; supplements may be beneficial for certain individuals if recommended by their doctor.

Exercise is another important aspect of senior health that should not be overlooked when investing in health and wellness programs for seniors.

Regular physical activity has been proven to boost energy levels, strengthen bones & muscles, reduce stress levels, improve balance & coordination, prevent falls, lower blood pressure & cholesterol levels.

Seniors should focus on low-impact activities such as walking, swimming, yoga or tai chi which are all good options depending on individual ability level.

Additionally, joining group classes at local gyms or recreation centers will provide motivation from others along with professional instruction from certified trainers who can tailor exercises specifically towards the needs of each individual senior participant.

Social engagement is also essential when it comes to maintaining mental wellbeing among older adults; studies have shown that loneliness increases the risk factors associated with developing dementia so, staying connected through meaningful relationships is very important. Senior centers offer many different types of recreational activities where people can meet new friends including card games, bingo, book clubs, cooking classes, art classes etc.

Social media sites are also popular amongst older generations allowing them to connect virtually with family members living far away without having to leave home making it easier than ever before to keep up long distance relationships.

Finally investing money into preventive healthcare services like annual checkups, vaccinations, vision, and hearing tests are extremely important to ensuring any medical issues caught early enough, and treated properly, can avoid becoming more serious problems later down road. This investment could potentially save a lot of time, hassle and money while preventing hospitalizations, unnecessary surgeries, and medical complications.

All these investments combined would create a comprehensive holistic approach toward keeping the elderly population safe, happy, and healthy during longer periods of time resulting in them enjoying their lives to the fullest extent possible.

CHAPTER 11
EDUCATION THROUGH ONLINE COURSES

I n today's world, the importance of developing new skills and staying up to date with technology is paramount for seniors. With the advent of online courses, it has become much easier for seniors to learn new skills and stay abreast of current trends in their field.

As previously touched upon, online courses provide an ideal solution for those who don't have time or the resources to attend a traditional classroom setting. Online courses are cost-effective and highly accessible; they can be taken from anywhere with an internet connection at any time that suits the learner's schedule.

This makes them ideal for seniors who may not always be able to leave home or travel far distances due to physical constraints.

Additionally, online learning platforms often offer flexible payment options which make taking these classes more affordable than attending regular college classes.

Seniors should take advantage of online course offerings as they provide a great opportunity for self-improvement in various areas such as computer science, business management, health care administration and many others.

For example, if a senior wants to gain expertise in web design but lacks basic coding knowledge then he/she can easily find an introductory HTML & CSS course on any popular eLearning platform like Udemy or Coursera without having to leave home or attend classroom sessions regularly. Similarly, if someone wishes to brush up on their public speaking skills then there are plenty of communication workshops available on these forums also.

Moreover, most eLearning sites offer certificates after completion of each course which adds an extra layer of credibility when applying for jobs or seeking promotions within one's existing organization, something that might otherwise be difficult (or expensive) for older adults trying out something completely new late in life.

Finally, yet importantly, taking part in online courses provides seniors with a sense of accomplishment and purpose during retirement years, something that cannot be achieved by simply sitting idle at home all day long! It gives them access to information about modern technologies which helps to keep them stay engaged intellectually while allowing them to continue contributing positively towards society even after retiring from work life officially!

CHAPTER 12
EXPLORING SENIOR LIVING COMMUNITIES

Senior living communities are a great way for seniors to remain active and independent, while also having access to health care services, social activities, and other amenities. Seniors who are looking into senior living communities should take the time to explore their options to find the right fit for them.

The first step in exploring senior living communities is researching what types of facilities are available. There are many different types of senior living facilities such as assisted living facilities, memory care units, continuing care retirement centers (CCRCs), nursing homes, and skilled nursing homes.

Each facility offers different levels of care depending on individual needs. Researching each type can help seniors determine which one will best suit their lifestyle and needs.

Once a specific type has been chosen, it's important for seniors to visit several different locations within that category before deciding about where they want to live. Visiting multiple places allows them to get an idea of the atmosphere at each community so they can pick one that fits with their personality and interests best.

They should ask questions about staff qualifications, safety features, cost of services provided including meals or transportation costs if applicable, and any additional amenities offered like fitness centers or recreational activities. Knowing all these details ahead of time will make choosing a home much easier once everything is taken into consideration. Seniors should also consider how close family members may be able to visit when selecting a location; some senior housing complexes offer special discounts for family members who come more often than others do!

Additionally, if possible, seniors should talk with current residents at each potential location in order get an honest opinion on life there from someone who lives there day-to-day.

This could provide valuable insight into whether this would be the right place for them long-term! After narrowing down choices based on research and visits, it's important that seniors to review all contracts carefully before signing anything.

All contracts should include information regarding move-in fees, monthly rent payments, medical services included (if any), and cancellation policies amongst other things. Moreover, it's vital that seniors read through every line carefully because contracts vary from place to place even within same type/kind of community; so, understanding what exactly you 're paying for is very crucial prior to committing yourself legally!

Lastly but most importantly don't hesitate to seek professional advice if needed when navigating through your search process as well as during finalization stage especially if there are financially related matters involved! Financial advisors or lawyer might come handy here offering guidance throughout the entire process helping you make wise decisions towards safe future planning! Exploring senior living communities can be overwhelming but taking steps listed above can ensure finding perfect fit both financially & emotionally speaking thus allowing everyone to enjoy their golden years peacefully without worries!

CHAPTER 13
SENIORS EMBRACING TECHNOLOGY

With the rapid development of technology and digital media, many seniors may feel overwhelmed trying to keep up with today's digital age. However, there are many ways for seniors to stay connected and engaged in this new era.

First, it is important for seniors to become comfortable using their devices such as Smartphone's or tablets. Many of these devices come with user-friendly interfaces that make learning how to use them easier than ever before. It can be helpful for seniors to take a class on how to use their device or watch tutorials online so they can learn at their own pace.

Once they are familiar with the basics, such as sending texts and emails or searching the internet, then more advanced features like downloading apps or streaming music will become easier too! Second, social media platforms provide a great way for seniors to stay connected with friends and family members who live far away.

As previously discussed, platforms such as Face book or Instagram offer easy-to-use options that allow users of all ages and backgrounds to connect quickly without having any technical knowledge beforehand.

Additionally, most platforms have safety settings that can help protect against potential scams or other malicious activity while giving users control over what content they post online. Thirdly, utilizing video conferencing software like Facetime, Skype or Zoom is a great way for senior citizens to stay in touch with loved ones near and far since it allows multiple people from different locations around the world to join into one virtual call together easily. This is something unheard of just decades ago! Video calls also give an extra layer of personalization when compared to regular phone calls since participants can see each other's facial expressions which helps create stronger connections between two parties even if separated by distance.

Finally, taking advantage of educational opportunities available through websites such as Courser provides an excellent opportunity for older adults looking to gain skills needed in today's job market without leaving home!

By completing courses on topics ranging from computer programming languages all the way up through complex topics like Artificial Intelligence (AI), anyone regardless of age has access to high quality education materials taught by experts in their respective field's free-of-charge via their web browsers anywhere around the globe provided there is internet connection available nearby.

By understanding some basic principles about modern technology along with taking advantage of resources readily available out there today, seniors can easily keep up with today's digital age no matter where they might be located physically speaking.

With this newfound confidence, aging individuals now have greater ability to explore everything that the world wide web has to offer them including but not limited to, staying connected socially or engaging in educational pursuits or growing personally or culturally.

CHAPTER 14
SENIORS TRAVELING AROUND THE WORLD

As the world has become more accessible to everyone, seniors are now taking advantage of their retirement years by traveling around the world. From exploring new cultures and cuisines to discovering hidden gems, there's something for everyone when it comes to senior travel.

There are many advantages that come with being a senior traveler. With age comes wisdom, so seniors often have an easier time navigating unfamiliar places than younger travelers do. Seniors also tend to be better at budgeting and planning trips since they've likely had plenty of practice over the years. Plus, due to their age and experience, they usually receive discounts on airfares and accommodations.

One of the most important things for seniors embarking on a journey is safety. It pays off to plan where possible to avoid any potential risks or dangers during your travels. Research local laws before you go; make sure you know what documents you will need to enter certain countries; bring along enough medication (if needed); pack light but smartly; keep your valuables secure; take out travel insurance.

Stay alert while walking through busy streets or public places; be aware of scams that target tourists; always carry a phone with working data/internet connection if possible... Additionally, don't forget about health-related issues such as altitude sickness or dehydration which can affect anyone regardless of age.

So, factor this into your plans too! Additionally, best practices when it comes to senior travel include staying active during your trip by engaging in activities like sightseeing tours.

This helps maintain fitness levels throughout the duration of your trip as well as providing insight into cultural customs and traditions from locals who may provide tips on where else you should visit while you are abroad! Other great ideas include joining organized group tours. These can offer company and security during solo travels plus some groups even feature special discounted rates for seniors!

Finally ensure that all necessary vaccinations & immunizations have been taken prior to your departure date especially if travelling internationally. This will reduce your risk significantly when visiting foreign lands abroad!

Overall travelling around the world provides exciting opportunities for exploration and growth at any stage in life including those in later stages too!

If done right seniors can enjoy incredible experiences without compromising safety or comfort levels thanks largely to advances made within the tourism industry that specifically caters towards older generations today!

CHAPTER 15
SENIORS AND SOCIAL MEDIA NETWORKING

In today's world, social media has become an essential part of our lives. It is used for a variety of purposes such as networking, finding jobs and staying connected with friends and family. Seniors can also take advantage of the various platforms available to help them to stay active socially and professionally.

While earlier chapters have touched on this subject, the most important thing for seniors to understand about using social media for networking is that it takes time and effort. The key is to be consistent in posting content that will attract others who are interested in similar topics or activities.

This could include anything from sharing photos of hobbies or interests to writing blog posts related to current events or experiences. By being proactive on these sites, seniors can start building relationships with people they may not otherwise have access to without the help of technology.

Another great way seniors can use social media platforms for networking purposes is by engaging with other users in meaningful conversations through comments sections or direct messages. This allows them to get their point across while also learning more about what other people think on certain topics or events happening around the world.

Additionally, this kind of interaction helps build trust between individuals which makes it easier for potential employers or business contacts to take notice when considering someone for a job opportunity or partnership venture down the line.

Additionally, many successful professionals use LinkedIn as a platform specifically designed for career-oriented networking opportunities; thus, making it an ideal place for seniors looking into new roles within their field after retirement age sets in.

On this site they are able showcase their work history and skillet while connecting with former colleagues and peers who might be able to offer advice on how best approach these types of opportunities when they arise back up again later down the road.

Furthermore, joining groups relevant to your industry of interest can help you keep informed of the various trends so that one day, if the need arises, you already have a knowledge base prepared to utilize.

Finally, utilizing Twitter, or "X' as it is now known, should not be overlooked either as its popularity continues to increase amongst all generations due its ability to easily spread information quickly far wide. For example, one tweet from an influencer regarding a certain topic can spark conversations between thousands or even millions of followers creating huge potential exposure for anyone involved.

Therefore, those seeking to gain more publicity can benefit greatly from participating within the "X" sphere since there is a good chance of you having your voice heard among the masses at any given moment in time.

Overall, senior citizens should make sure they familiarize themselves with the tools available so they may benefit from this new modern digital age that we all live in now these days.

There are countless ways to network, both on a personal and professional level, via the internet. But it requires dedication to maintain your online presence consistently to reap the rewards.

CHAPTER 16
SENIORS AND GENERATIONAL RELATIONSHIPS

I n recent years, intergenerational relationships have become increasingly important for seniors. As the population ages and more people are living longer lives, building meaningful relationships with members of other generations is a great way to stay connected and engaged in the world around them. Intergenerational relationships provide seniors with an opportunity to learn from different experiences and perspectives, gain fresh insight into life's challenges, and share their own wisdom. Intergenerational relationships can be beneficial for both parties involved. Not only do they allow seniors to feel valued as an integral part of society but also help younger generations develop an understanding about ageism and how they can support our elders.

The benefits of these connections go beyond mere companionship; there are many tangible advantages that come from forming strong intergenerational bonds such as improved physical health, mental wellbeing, social engagement, reduced loneliness, or depression symptoms.

One of the most significant aspects of intergenerational interactions is that it enables older adults to pass down knowledge accumulated over a lifetime; this could include anecdotes about past events or lessons learned through experience which may not be available elsewhere.

Seniors who engage in conversations with young people can draw on their own personal stories which can often be inspiring for those listening - providing motivation for tackling difficult tasks or achieving goals once thought impossible!

In addition, sharing one's skillet allows younger generations to benefit from having access to expertise that would otherwise take time (and money) to acquire themselves like teaching someone how to knit or cook.

Furthermore, learning together creates lasting memories between two individuals regardless of the difference in age. This condition significantly invites mutual respect while engaging in each individual's best interest making everyone feel equal no matter what generation they belong too!

Moreover, research has shown that senior citizens who form close friendships with younger peers tend to have better emotional well-being than those without any connection whatsoever due solely based on factoring out things such as gender/ethnicity or socioeconomic status.

This is because when interacting across generational divides there's less likely chance, you'll encounter prejudice against your age group, so it helps to combat a feeling of being isolated or discriminated against. Plus, it also gives a greater sense of belonging within the community overall! Additionally, spending quality time doing activities together provides opportunities that build trustworthiness between two people regardless of where they stand in terms of life stage or experience.

Ultimately this results in a stronger bond overall. All things considered, developing intergenerational relationships should be encouraged among senior citizens due its various positive effects on physical health, mental wellbeing (reduce depression symptoms), social engagement and increased sense of belonging within the community.

Plus, passing down lifelong knowledge and skill sets onto the next future generations is important so that nothing is lost or forgotten will be a great benefit.

CHAPTER 17
SENIOR EDUCATIONAL
OPPORTUNITIES

S enior educational opportunities refer to courses, programs, and activities that are specifically designed for seniors. These opportunities can provide a wide range of benefits for those who take advantage of them. They help people stay up to date with current trends in their field or area of interest. They help develop new skills and knowledge. They help to socialize with peers, remain active mentally and physically, and gain access to important resources they may not have had.

While this topic was also touched upon earlier, I thought it was important enough to expand upon it. One type of senior educational opportunity is taking classes at a local college or university. Many institutions offer special discounts on tuition fees for seniors or allow them to audit certain classes without paying tuition fees. In addition to being able to learn new things in traditional classroom settings, many colleges also offer online courses which can be taken from the comfort of one's home.

This makes it much more accessible than attending physical classes on campus due to transportation issues or other limitations associated with getting around at an advanced age.

Another option available is participating in lifelong learning programs offered by organizations such as Elderhostel (now Road Scholar). These types of programs combine travel experiences with seminars taught by experts in various fields so that participants can explore topics like history, science and culture while gaining valuable knowledge about the subject matter at hand. Additionally, these trips often include plenty of sightseeing which makes them ideal for retirees looking for something fun and stimulating to do during their golden years!

Other senior educational opportunities involve joining adult education centers where seniors can attend lectures or workshops covering a variety of topics ranging from art appreciation to computer literacy depending upon what interests them most.

Many centers also organize day trips out into nature so that participants get some fresh air while enjoying the company of others in their own age group as well as knowledgeable guides who will teach them about plants and animals along the way! Finally, there are volunteer positions available through organizations like AARP that allow seniors to use their talents towards helping causes that they care deeply about while developing relationships within the community they live in, all while learning something new every day!

No matter what type of senior educational opportunity someone decides is best suited for themselves whether it's taking classes at college, exploring distant lands via Elderhostel; attending lectures/workshops at an adult education center; or volunteering, these kinds of activities are invaluable when it comes to providing individuals over 55 years old with mental stimulation, socialization options and even career development possibilities if desired! In the end, life is a precious gift, a journey filled with beauty and wonder, and an opportunity to create a legacy that reflects the depth and richness of our souls. And for seniors, there is no better time to embrace the beauty and wonder of life, to live each day with courage, curiosity, and joy.

By embracing life, seniors can create a legacy that reflects the beauty and wonder of their lives and find comfort and support in the love and companionship of others. So, let's embrace the power of life, and let's live each day with a heart full of gratitude and wonder.

As you look back on your life, with all its ups and downs, you may start to wonder what you've lost and what you've found. But let me tell you, my dear friend, that age is just a number.

There's so much you can still achieve and so many ways to remain relevant. The world may seem daunting, but don't let that deter you.

You still have so much to give and so much to pursue. Remember, it's never too late to chase your dreams and goals. The world needs your wisdom and experience, and your unique, valuable soul.

So don't ever think that you're too old, or that your time has passed. The best is yet to come, my friend, and you can make it last.

Keep your heart open and your mind sharp, and never stop learning and growing. You have so much to offer the world, and so much more worth knowing. Stay relevant, stay engaged, and always stay true to you. The world is yours to conquer, and your potential is far from through.

MY PERSONAL JOURNEY

"Everyone gets to be young, but not everyone gets to be old."
Anonymous

"It's one thing to write about how to remain relevant or give advice about the subject. In that regard, I thought I would add this section of my book to discuss my personal journey to try and stay relevant as I began to reach the senior years of my life. At 86, I hope my story will serve as an example or proof that staying and remaining relevant has no age boundaries."

At 59 years old, and after having gone through a second heartbreaking divorce, I found myself back in the single world again. Throughout the nearly 21 years that I was married, I had been an avid tennis player. My wife also played tennis and we would often play with married friends.

Tennis was a major part of our lives. In addition to belonging to a tennis club we also had a tennis court at our home in Westlake Village where we would often host tennis tournaments for our friends and other members of the tennis club that we belonged to.

But first, some earlier background. After returning from Military service and up until I moved to California from New Jersey in 1971, with my young family, I had studied Guitar and was enamored with the jazz style of music.

I had studied with Sal Salvatore, guitarist with the Stan Kenton big band, and later with the legendary jazz guitarist, Harry Leahy.

During that time period, I also had a big job working in New York in the financial district. However, every weekend I also had a steady job playing guitar in a jazz quartet that was the house band at the Sterrington Catering House in Montclair, New Jersey.

For nearly 5 years I played with the other group of jazz musicians and enjoyed having a dual career. In 1971, I received an extraordinary opportunity from a major financial company to move to California and head up the company's western marketing operations. This was a big job and a big opportunity for my career.

My two children were very young, but I realized my focus had to now be on my family and their financial welfare.

I also knew it would mean me giving up the band that I had been working with for the past 5 years. I also had to consider how much my new workload and responsibilities would affect my music career.

In 1971, I received an extraordinary opportunity from a major financial company to move to California and head up the company's western marketing operations. This was a big job and a big opportunity for my career.

My two children were very young, but I realized my focus had to now be on my family and their financial welfare. I also knew it would mean me giving up the band that I had been working with for the past 5 years. I also had to consider how much my new workload and responsibilities would affect my music career.

In June of 1971 I moved to California, lock, stock, and barrel with my wife and two little children to pursue the "American Dream".

As time went by, I picked up my guitar only on occasion until finally, after a year or so, I stopped playing completely. With the result of moving across the country to what seemed like a different world, and the rigors of a new job and the responsibilities of overseeing 160 employees, I looked to a new outlet to balance the stress and anxieties my marriage and of my new position. I took up the sport of tennis.

Tennis was a Godsend as it helped me to stay in shape physically and take my mind off my Job and the marriage difficulties I was experiencing because of my moving to California.

By the end of my second year in California, America was going through recession and the company I had been working for began laying off their employees. It was a slow process.

Eventually, I received my severance pay, which ended my new career with the company that brought me to California. It also ended my marriage of 9 years. As a result of the OPEC oil embargo that was causing high gas prices and shortages resulting in long lines at the pumps, I decided to go into the domestic oil and gas business. Along with an attorney who had also worked for the company that I had left; we formed a company called "Tri-Star Oil & Gas" with the objective of taking advantage of the generous tax codes for oil and gas exploration by raising capital from wealthy investors for domestic oil and gas projects. During that same period, I met a woman who I later married.

Over the next 20+ years and up until my divorce at 59, my focus was on playing tennis and the successful business enterprises I had created, which were now either sold or taken over by others. Finding myself single again, with my kids grown, being a grandfather and facing the years ahead as a senior citizen, I thought "what did the future hold"? How could I stay relevant in the world that was rapidly changing around me? My children remembered that earlier in my life I had been a musician. They suggested that I take an interest in music again.

I thought that might be a good Idea. I always had a piano around the house for the kids or guests who would visit and sit and play. So, rather than picking up the guitar again, I decided that I would learn to play the piano.

Fortunately, I had a musical background having played the guitar professionally for many years. The problem that I was facing was developing the fingering facility to play, learning the various scales and the hours of practice that would be required to become a competent piano player. This would be my challenge.

By the time I was 63, I had become competent enough as a jazz pianist to begin performing publicly. My family was stunned by what I had achieved by my efforts to remain relevant.

For 2 ½ years I was the house piano player at Ritrovo's restaurant in Westlake Village, California It didn't stop there. The Internet was just becoming a big deal. Websites were springing all over.

The E-Commerce industry was emerging at a rapid pace. It seemed that everyone was getting into it. It was an exciting time and I wanted to be part of it. At that time my son-in-law was the president of a major toy company manufacturer. I found out that his company was not selling retail on the internet. An idea occurred to me. Would his company allow me to sell their toys on the internet through an E- Commerce website?

I was given the green light. However, I did not know how to build an E-Commerce website. As a result, I enrolled at the Conejo Valley Adult Education night school where I learned how to build a website using Adobe's "Dreamweaver" software. I went 3 nights a week for one month and received my certified certificate of completion. I proceeded to develop my website and my online business called, "Speedy dog" *Delivering toys to your doorstep fast!*

For the next 7 years I remained relevant selling and shipping thousands of toys that resulted through my online "Speedydog" website. I was now in my 70's when I closed the business down because of competition from Amazon.

At the time I closed the business down I was witnessing a new and more comprehensive digital business model emerging. It was at a holiday party that by happenstance I would meet an old buddy of mine who told me about a Business he was creating in the field of Digital Marketing. Our conversations led to forming a business alignment between us. We began working together to create a business plan that would include green screen live video presentations, website development, and creating and promoting marketing materials and professional videos for businesses.

During the time we were together, we jointly wrote a number one best-selling book in 2014 on Amazon called, "Rise above the cloud with Digital Marketing", which can be purchased on Amazon.

At 79, I moved out of California and moved to Colorado to be with my daughter, husband and their 4 children.

Two of my grandchildren were enrolled in universities there. I was there for a year when I created my own online Digital Marketing Company called, MedialineInteractive .com However, being used to California weather, I found the Colorado winter much too cold for me, so I moved to Boca Raton, Florida, where many of my family members live close by.

It was 2017 when I arrived in Florida. I was 80 years old. My cousins, being aware of my marketing and digital skills, offered me a part-time job in their trucking company as their Marketing Director. Thankful to being able to stay relevant at this time in my life, I accepted and proceeded to build a brand-new unique website for them. Over the next 5 years I continued to manage their website and other duties.

In addition, I was happy playing piano regularly at various establishments and at private parties. In the meantime, my grandchildren upon graduating had decided, along with my daughter and husband, to move back to Santa Barbara, California.

This presented a problem for me as I was now 85, with a good job, playing piano and living in Boca Raton. My daughter, concerned with my age, insisted that I return to California and live nearby.

In April 2023, I returned to California. I moved into Friendship Manor, a retirement community in Goleta, California at the foothills of the Santa Yanez Mountains, three blocks from the ocean. I live 4 miles away from my daughter and grandchildren. I see them often, which makes me happy. My son lives in Las Vegas.

We face time each other a few times a week. As I approach my 86th birthday, I am thankful that I continue to manage my cousin's website remotely while being available for any other task that they may have me do. I continue to play the piano and collaborate with many of the talented musicians who live here at Friendship Manor.

I've written this book and as the author, I have included my personal journey. I hope somewhere in these pages my own experience will light a flame and shed a light on how you too can remain productive, happy, and most importantly, remain…

"RELEVANT"

Made in the USA
Las Vegas, NV
17 May 2024

90047241R00059